Milet Publishing
Smallfields Cottage, Cox Green
Rudgwick, Horsham, West Sussex
RH12 3DE England
info@milet.com
www.milet.com
www.milet.co.uk

First English–Russian edition published by Milet Publishing in 2013

Copyright © Milet Publishing, 2013

ISBN 978 1 84059 814 8

Original Turkish text written by Erdem Seçmen
Translated to English by Alvin Parmar and adapted by Milet

Illustrated by Chris Dittopoulos
Designed by Christangelos Seferiadis

Printed and bound in Turkey by Ertem Matbaası

My Bilingual Book

Smell
Обоняние

English–Russian

How do you smell a garden of flowers?

Как узнать запах свежести после дождя,

Or the fresh air after rain showers?

Ощутить аромат, в сад цветущий входя?

Smell is one of our senses, as you know.

Обоняние – наше чувство, и так повелось:

It's the reason you have a nose!

Чтобы запах узнать, нам нужен нос.

Like hearing, sight, taste, and touch,

Словно зрение, слух, вкус, осязание, –

your sense of smell tells you so much.

Нам так много рассказывает обоняние!

It helps you decide what you like to eat,

Нос подскажет, что взял на обед ты с собой…

and animals you don't want to meet!

Или что рядом зверь: обойди стороной!

Your nose is your detective for finding cakes.

Нос, словно сыщик, находит пирог.

It will track down goodies, whatever it takes!

Спрятать сласти от носа никто бы не смог!

Your smell sense tells you where you are,

Обоняние подскажет, где же ты есть:

in a forest, by the sea, or in a city full of cars!

В лесу, у моря, или там, где машин не счесть.

There are so many smells that we enjoy,

Многим нравится, как пахнут хлеб или мыло,

like soap and bread and our best cuddly toy!

У любимой игрушки запах премилый!

When you smell yourself and say, oh my gosh!

Иногда ты по запаху сможешь понять,

You know it's time for a really good wash!

Что пора бы тебе ванну принять!

A cold makes your nose stuffy and red,

Если насморк, заложенный нос покраснеет.

but it will get better if you rest in bed.

Значит, лучше тебе отлежаться в постели.

And once you are well,

А когда восстановишь ты свои силы,

go out and smell!

Выходи на природу, ощути запах мира!